D0771170

Let's Celebrate Freedom!

THE UNITED STATES CONSTITUTION AND THE BILL OF RIGHTS

Lorijo Metz

PowerKiDS press

New York

Dedicated to my father, Joe Rush – Our Family's Founding Father

Published in 2014 by The Rosen Publishing Group, Inc.
29 East 21st Street, New York, NY 10010

Copyright © 2014 by The Rosen Publishing Group, Inc.

All rights reserved. No part of this book may be reproduced in any form without permission in writing from the publisher, except by a reviewer.

First Edition

Editor: Amelie von Zumbusch
Book Design: Colleen Bialecki
Photo Research: Katie Stryker

Photo Credits: Cover Superstock/Getty Images; pp. 4, 7, 13 (top) , 9 (top) Library of Congress Prints and Photographs Division Washington, D.C.; p. 5 David McNew/Staff/Getty Images News/Getty Images; pp. 8, 12, 21 iStockphoto/Thinkstock; p. 11 Tom Williams/Contributor/CQ-Roll Call Group/Getty Images; p. 13 (bottom) zimmytws/Shutterstock.com; p. 14 Katherine Welles/Shutterstock.com; p. 15 AFP/Stringer/Getty Images; p. 17 Eric Crama/Shutterstock.com; p. 18 Andre Blais/Shutterstock.com; p. 19 Stephen Coburn/Shutterstock.com; p. 20 Buyenlarge/Contributor/Archive Photos/Getty Images; p. 22 paulaphoto/Shutterstock.com.

Library of Congress Cataloging-in-Publication Data

Metz, Lorijo.
  The United States Constitution and the Bill of Rights / By Lorijo Metz. — First edition.
      pages cm. — (Let's celebrate freedom!)
  Includes index.
  ISBN 978-1-4777-2895-6 (library) — ISBN 978-1-4777-2984-7 (pbk.) —
  ISBN 978-1-4777-3054-6 (6-pack)
  1. United States. Constitution—Juvenile literature. 2. Constitutional history—United States—Juvenile literature.
  3. Constitutional law—United States–Juvenile literature. I. Title.
  E303.M54 2013
  342.7302'9—dc23
                                    2013021793

Manufactured in the United States of America

CPSIA Compliance Information: Batch # W14PK4: For Further Information contact Rosen Publishing, New York, New York at 1-800-237-9932

CONTENTS

WE THE PEOPLE

In 1783, the American Revolution officially ended. The United States had won its independence from Great Britain. To remain free, however, the people needed a stronger government to keep them **united**. They did not want another king. Instead, they created a new government, in which the people elected their leaders.

This painting shows the end of the Battle of Trenton. It was part of the American Revolution, which happened when 13 British colonies rebelled against Great Britain.

One of the rights that the Bill of Rights protects is "the right of the people peaceably to assemble." This right covers protests such as the one seen here.

The US Constitution, created in 1787, sets out how our government works. For the first time in history, it limited the powers of the **federal**, or central, government. The Bill of Rights was added to the Constitution in 1791. It **protects** personal rights, such as freedom of speech and religion.

A WEAK START

During the American Revolution, the 13 original states united under a weak central government. Representatives **ratified**, or approved, the **Articles** of Confederation in 1781. Under them, each state created its own money and laws, making trade between them difficult. When the US government needed to pay the soldiers who had fought in the revolution, it had to beg the states for money.

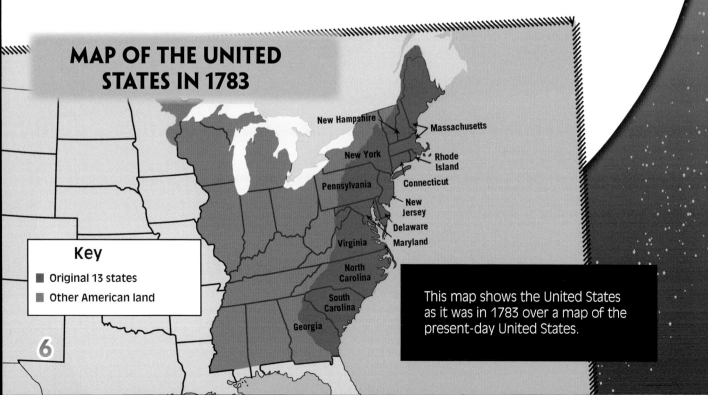

MAP OF THE UNITED STATES IN 1783

New Hampshire

Massachusetts

New York

Rhode Island

Connecticut

Pennsylvania

New Jersey

Delaware

Virginia

Maryland

North Carolina

South Carolina

Georgia

Key

■ Original 13 states

■ Other American land

This map shows the United States as it was in 1783 over a map of the present-day United States.

The members of the Constitutional Convention elected George Washington the convention's president.

The central government was so weak that some Americans began to worry that their new nation would not survive. In 1787, American leaders held a meeting in Philadelphia, Pennsylvania, to talk about ways to address these problems. The meeting became known as the Constitutional Convention.

A MORE PERFECT UNION

Leaders from 12 of the 13 states attended the Constitutional Convention. Rather than fix the Articles of Confederation, the leaders came up with a new **document**, the Constitution. Under it, states shared power with the federal government. Among the Constitution's main authors was James Madison from Virginia.

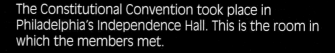

The Constitutional Convention took place in Philadelphia's Independence Hall. This is the room in which the members met.

Madison is considered a Founding Father, or man who helped set up and shape the United States. In 1808, he was elected the fourth president of the United States.

Only nine states needed to ratify the Constitution to make it official. On June 21, 1789, New Hampshire leaders ratified it by a narrow vote. The Constitution became the law of the land! As the **preamble**, or opening words, of the Constitution explains, it was written "in order to form a more perfect union."

The Constitution has seven articles that explain how the government works. The first three articles explain the three branches of the government. These branches set up a system of checks and balances. Each branch keeps the others in check so that no branch can become too powerful.

Article I describes the legislative branch, or Congress, which makes the laws. Congress includes the Senate and House of Representatives. Article II covers the executive branch, which makes sure the laws are carried out. The president is the head of the executive branch. Article III explains the judicial branch, including the **Supreme** Court, which makes important **legal** decisions.

Here you can see Congress gathered, along with several Supreme Court justices (bottom left) and the president (bottom right). All three branches of the federal government are represented.

11

TIMELINE

September 3, 1783

The Treaty of Paris is signed, ending the American Revolution.

September 17, 1787

After months of debate, 39 delegates sign the Constitution.

1779   1780   1781   1782   1783   1784   1785

May 25, 1787

The Constitutional Convention starts in Philadelphia.

April 30, 1789

George Washington becomes the first president of the United States of America.

December 15, 1791

Virginia becomes the tenth and final state needed to ratify the Bill of Rights.

| 1786 | 1787 | 1788 | 1789 | 1790 | 1791 | 1792 |

June 21, 1788

New Hampshire ratifies the Constitution, making it the law of the land.

May 29, 1790

Rhode Island becomes the thirteenth and final state to ratify the Constitution.

FOUR FINAL ARTICLES

Article IV concerns the states. It explains how new states can join the Union. It says all states must honor the laws of other states. It also covers how the federal government treats the states, including protecting them in times of war. Article V explains how **amendments**, or changes, can be made to the Constitution.

The first new state to join the Union after the original 13 was Vermont. It became a state in 1791. This photo shows Vermont's capital, Montpelier, as it looks today.

Presidents swear the oath of office at the very beginning of their terms. In the oath, they promise to "preserve, protect and defend the Constitution of the United States."

Article VI establishes the Constitution as the supreme, or highest, law of the land. It also says no one running for public office, such as president, will have to pass a religious test. The seventh article explains that only nine states needed to ratify the Constitution for it to become law.

THE BILL OF RIGHTS

Shortly after the Constitution became law, James Madison wrote twelve amendments. Ten of them went on to become the Bill of Rights. The First Amendment says that citizens may worship as they please. They may say or write what they want and may meet peacefully in groups. Also, the government must listen to their complaints.

James Madison believed the country needed a **militia**, or national guard, for protection. The Second Amendment gives citizens the right to own guns. The Third Amendment says that citizens do not have to house soldiers unless the government makes a special law during a war.

The right to gather in peaceful groups is also known as the freedom of assembly.

OTHER IMPORTANT RIGHTS

The Fourth Amendment says police may not arrest citizens or search their homes without a **warrant**, or approval from a judge. The Fifth Amendment protects the rights of citizens accused of crimes, while the sixth promises them the right to a lawyer and a fair trial by jury.

Since the Constitution shares power between the federal government and the states, states can have different laws about certain things. For example, you can drive at different ages in different states.

One of the things that the Fifth Amendment says is that people accused of crimes cannot be made to testify, or speak, against themselves at their trials.

The Seventh Amendment guarantees that if one citizen sues another for more than $20, that person has the right to a trial by jury. The Eighth Amendment explains that all fines and punishments for crimes must be fair. The Ninth Amendment says citizens may have other rights that must be protected. The Tenth Amendment says that powers not given to the federal government belong to the states.

LATER AMENDMENTS

The Bill of Rights promised to protect citizens' rights. It would be many years, however, before the US government treated all men and women, no matter their race, equally under the law.

The right to vote is known as suffrage. The women here took part in a parade supporting women's suffrage in New York City in 1912.

The Supreme Court outlawed separating black and white students in 1954. Its decision rested on the Fourteenth Amendment. The court case started at Monroe Elementary School in Topeka, Kansas.

In 1865, the Thirteenth Amendment outlawed slavery. In 1868, the Fourteenth Amendment promised American citizens of all races equal protection under the law. In 1870, the Fifteenth Amendment said that no man could be refused the right to vote based on race, color, or the fact that he had once been a slave. In 1920, women finally won the right to vote when Tennessee became the final state needed to ratify the Nineteenth Amendment.

INSPIRING FREEDOM

Before 1787, most people could not imagine a large nation without a king. Today, almost all of the roughly 200 countries in the world have constitutions. The US Constitution has lasted the longest. It has inspired nearly all of the constitutions that came after, from the 1791 French Constitution to the 1999 Constitution of Nigeria.

The US Constitution continues to grow and change. Every year, people suggest new amendments. Currently there are 27 amendments. The twenty-sixth, added in 1971, gave 18-year-olds the right to vote!

The Constitution and Bill of Rights are the basis for the freedoms that all Americans, young and old, enjoy.

GLOSSARY

amendments (uh-MEND-ments) Additions or changes to the Constitution.

articles (AR-tih-kulz) Numbered parts of a piece of writing.

document (DOK-yoo-ment) A written or printed statement that gives official information about something.

federal (FEH-duh-rul) Having to do with the central government.

legal (LEE-gul) Having to do with the law.

militia (muh-LIH-shuh) A group of people who are trained and ready to fight when needed.

preamble (PREE-am-bel) A statement of introduction.

protects (pruh-TEKTS) Keeps safe.

ratified (RA-tih-fyd) To have been approved officially.

supreme (suh-PREEM) Greatest in power or rank.

united (yoo-NYT-ed) Brought together to act as a single group.

warrant (WOR-ent) A piece of paper that gives someone the authority to do something.

INDEX

WEBSITES

Due to the changing nature of Internet links, PowerKids Press has developed an online list of websites related to the subject of this book. This site is updated regularly. Please use this link to access the list: www.powerkidslinks.com/lcf/consti/